S0-BCM-481

FLY GUY PRESENTS: SPACE

Tedd Arnold

Scholastic Inc.

To fellow Elmiran Eileen Collins,
the first woman to pilot and, later,
to command a U.S. space shuttle—T.A.

Photo credits:
Front cover (background): © pixelparticle/Shutterstock; cover (foreground): © Paul Prescott/Shutterstock; back cover (background): © Science Photo Library/SuperStock (RF); pp. 4–5 (background): photo by Dane Penland, © Smithsonian Institution NASM; pp. 6–7 (background): © Stocktrek/Getty Images (RF); pp. 8–9 (background): © Photo Researchers/NASA/Getty Images; p. 9 (center): © NASA; p. 10 (top): © Paul Prescott/Shutterstock; p. 10 (bottom): © NASA; p. 11 (top): © NASA; p. 11 (bottom): © NASA; pp. 12–13 (background): © Science Photo Library/SuperStock (RF); p. 12 (center left): © Science Source; p. 14 (top): © Science Source (re-use); p. 15 (top): © Getty Images (RF); p. 16 (top): © Jerry Lodriguss/Science Source; p. 16 (bottom): © Max Dannenbaum/Getty Images; p. 17 (top): © Stocktrek/Getty Images (RF); p. 17 (center right): © Detlev van Ravenswaay/Science Source; p. 17 (bottom left): © Stocktrek/Getty Images (RF); pp. 18–19 (background): © Stocktrek/Getty Images (RF); p. 18 (center): © NASA; p. 19 (center right): © NASA; pp. 20–21 (background): © Ian McKinnell /Getty Images; p. 20 (left): © Roger Ressmeyer/Corbis; p. 21 (top): © NASA; p. 22 (bottom left): © NASA; p. 22 (bottom right): © NASA; p. 23 (top left): © Getty Images; p. 23 (bottom): © World Perspectives/Getty Images; p. 24 (top left): © NASA; p. 24 (top right): © Time & Life Pictures/Getty Images; p. 24 (bottom left): © NASA; p. 25 (top left): © NASA; p. 25 (bottom left): © NASA; p. 26 (background): © Ian McKinnell/Getty Images; p. 27 (top left): © Alex Wild/Visuals Unlimited/Corbis; p. 27 (center left): © Popperfoto/Getty Images; p. 27 (bottom left): © Bettmann/Corbis; p. 28 (center): © Christophe Lehenaff/Getty Images; p. 29 (top): © Rufous/Shutterstock; p. 29 (bottom): © NASA; pp. 30–31 (background): © NASA; p. 31 (center): © NASA.

ISBN 978-0-545-56492-2

Copyright © 2013 by Tedd Arnold.

All rights reserved. Published by Scholastic Inc.
SCHOLASTIC and associated logos are trademarks and/or registered trademarks of Scholastic Inc.

20   17/0

Printed in the U.S.A.   40
First printing, September 2013

A boy had a pet fly named Fly Guy.
Fly Guy could say the boy's name —

One day, Buzz and Fly Guy were at the space museum (meu-ZEE-uhm).

"I want to fly into space when I grow up!" said Buzz.

"Yeah," said Buzz. "We can learn all about space right here!"

Space means everything in the universe
(YOO-nih-vurs). The universe is made up
of planets, stars, suns, moons, and much,
much more.

There are eight planets in our solar system:
Mercury, Venus, Earth, Mars, Jupiter,
Saturn, Uranus, and Neptune.

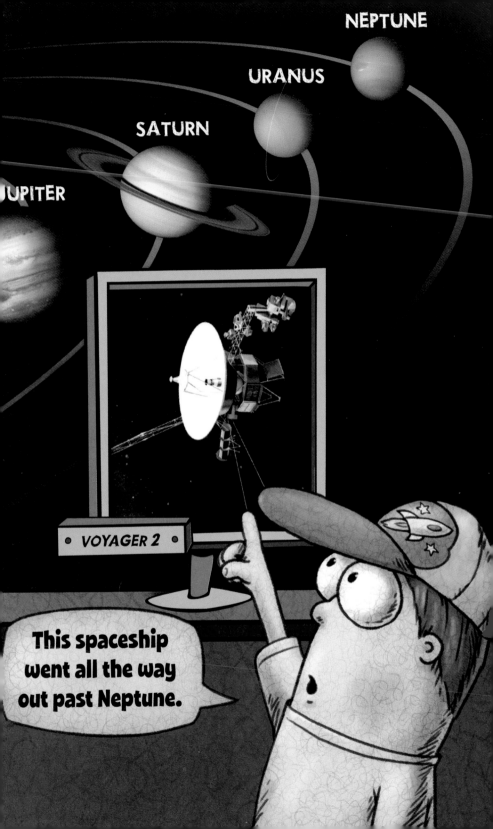

Moons orbit, or travel around, planets. Earth has one moon.

Earth and its moon

The surface of the Moon!

EARTH TO SCALE

The Sun is the biggest object in our solar system. It is 109 times wider than Earth!

The Sun's gravity pulls the planets like a giant magnet.

The Sun is the center of our solar system. All objects orbit around the Sun because it has gravity (GRAH-vih-tee). Gravity attracts objects to one another.

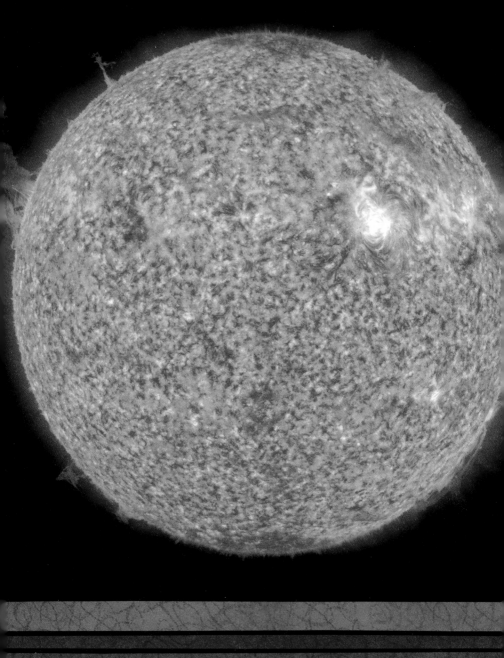

The Sun is a star. Stars are huge balls of
burning gas. Stars only look small because
they are so far away. The Sun is the close
star to Earth. It is 93 million miles away!

There are many other objects in our solar system.

Meteoroids (MEE-tee-uh-royds) are small rocks. When they fall toward Earth, they are called meteors (MEE-tee-uhrs).

A shooting star is really a meteor!

comet

Comets (KA-mets) are large pieces of rock, dust, and ice that orbit the Sun. Comets are called "dirty snowballs."

asteroid belt

asteroid

Asteroids (AS-tuh-royds) are made up of rock and metal. An asteroid belt is made up of lots of asteroids.

Astronauts are people who travel into space to find out more about it.

Astronauts call zero-gravity flights "vomit comets"!

ZERO·GRAVITY FLIGHT

There is no gravity or oxygen in space. Astronauts go on zero-gravity flights to learn how it feels to move without gravity. These rides are like very fast roller coasters!

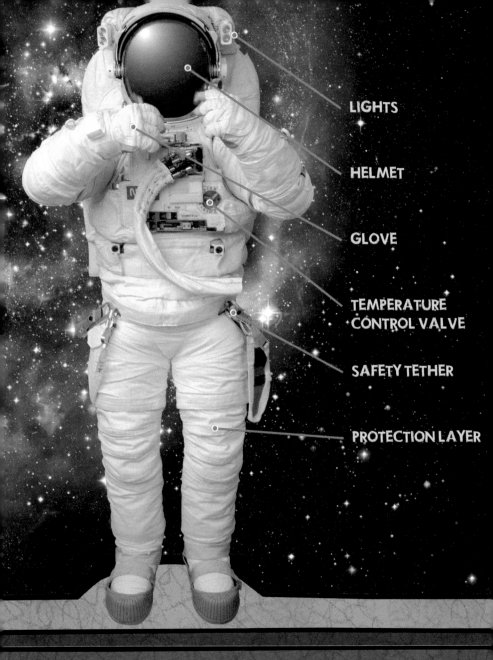

LIGHTS

HELMET

GLOVE

TEMPERATURE
CONTROL VALVE

SAFETY TETHER

PROTECTION LAYER

Astronauts wear special clothes to keep them safe. Space suits keep astronauts warm or cool and let them breathe.

A spacecraft is a vehicle that travels in space. There are many different types of spacecraft.

A space capsule is carried into space by a rocket. Some return to Earth by splashing down in water.

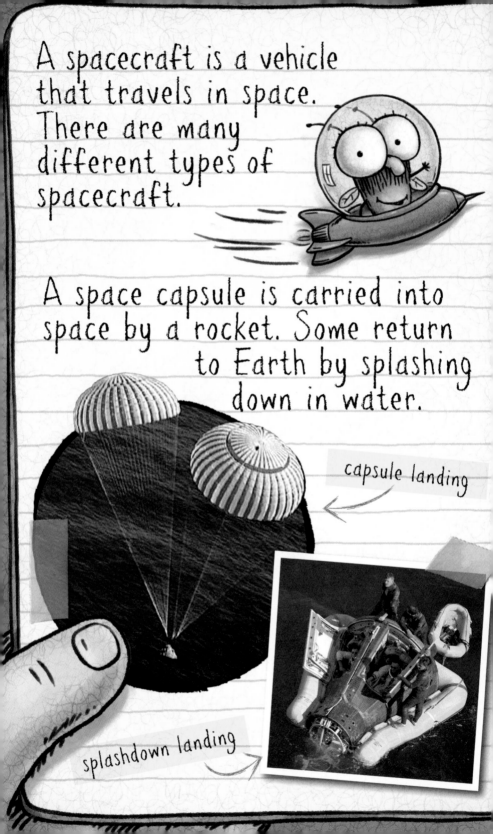

capsule landing

splashdown landing

A space shuttle also blasts off using rockets. When it returns to Earth, it lands on a runway like an airplane.

rocket boosters

space station

Astronauts can live on space stations. A space station can be as long and wide as a football field.

Astronauts have done amazing things!

1961

YURI GAGARIN

The first person in space.

1962

JOHN GLENN

The first American to orbit Earth.

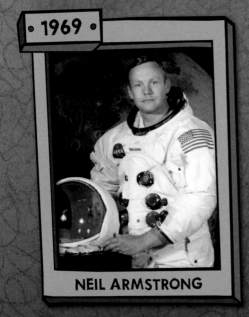

1969

NEIL ARMSTRONG

The first astronaut to walk on the Moon.

○ FIRST WORDS SAID ON THE MOON ○

"THE EAGLE HAS LANDED."

1986

**BARBARA MORGAN AND
CHRISTA McAULIFFE**

The first teachers
to be part of the
Teacher in Space
program.

1999

EILEEN COLLINS

The first woman
to command a
U.S. space shuttle.

Animals were sent into space before humans.

The first creatures
in space were
fruit flies.

Albert II became
the first monkey
in space.

A dog named
Laika became
the first animal
to orbit Earth.

Scientists can learn about space through telescopes. A telescope is a tool that uses lenses and mirrors to make faraway objects look nearer.

Look! Kids can use telescopes, too!

The Hubble Space Telescope is as big as a school bus!

There is still a lot to be learned about space. Earth is the only planet scientists know of that has living things on it. But scientists think there could be other life in the universe.

Mars Rovers are robots that explore Mars. Scientists are studying if there was ever water on Mars. If there was water there, there might have been life.

When Buzz got home, he made his very own asteroid belt.

Look, Fly Guy, I made it out of rocks and metal.

"We learned a lot about space today!" Buzz said. "I can't wait for our next field trip!"